Odes to life

Poems

Nicolás Muñoz -Muñoz

Original version in Spanish.
First English Edition. August 2024. Editorial 2020
Translation to English by the author. August 2024.
Edited by: Sophia Hernández. August 2024.

ISBN: 978-1-917317-25-2
Print: Amazon.
Cover design: Image created by AI

Contact for author: nmunoz50@gmail.com

Table of Contents

3

Dedication

I dedicate this book to my mentor in graduate studies in economics, the renowned Turkish economist and poet, Fuat Metin Andic. Fuat taught me that the study, teaching, and practice of economics and finance are not incompatible with the need to express your feelings and passions through poetry. Following Fuat's Passover in 2015, his wife, a distinguished economist, Dr. Suphan Andic, also my mentor, entrusted me with coordinating the publication of Fuat's unpublished poems in a posthumous collection, *Complete Turkish and Spanish Poems*. (Bibliográficas, San Juan, PR, 2017). Dr. Suphan Andic, as of the date of this publication (August 2024), lives in her residence in Washington DC., retired, wise, and enjoying her longevity.

Preface

Odes to Life first edition was in Spanish, my native language. This English language version is a translation adjusted to let the verses flow in English. The main reason for this effort is to let my grandchildren, nephews and nieces born or relocated in their early years to the mainland United States, who do not necessarily understand Spanish, enjoy my poetry. A second reason is to give access to the English-speaking community in the mainland USA, and the English-speaking world read my humble poetry. Amazon is the platform for this English edition publishing.

Odes to Life captures the essence of my emotional experiences throughout my life. Over the course of this life, I have traversed a path marked by the ups and downs of emotions, passions, and the complicated and lesser-known matters of existence. Although I do not consider myself a poet in the traditional sense, poetry has been my way of giving voice to those feelings that have filled my soul over the years. I did not dare to publish them for many years.

But now, in the autumn of my life, I have decided to gather every piece of paper, every electronic file, to refine the texts of old and new poems, to replace the old rhyme and thesaurus/dictionaries with new electronic grammar aids, and to publish them. Let no one feel offended or abandoned, for they are just an expression of relief.

Silvia Adela Kohan says in her Spanish edition book How Poetry is Written (Plaza Publishers – 1998) that "writing poetry is to connect with one's own space and let it show through. Its practice presupposes facing a form of knowledge and an exploration of personal identity. The secret to carrying it out consists of having confidence in the power of words; knowing that every word thrown onto the paper can contain the entire world."

I remember vividly my childhood, when the simple act of collecting water in gourds from the nearby spring was a ritual of connection with nature, a magical dance between man and Earth. I grew up in a neighborhood, an isolated community without basic services such as potable water, paved roads, or electricity, bordered by the river, without a bridge, crossing, walking over the creek stones, river silent witness of my restlessness and my youthful dreams. In several of the poems, the river is present. In that environment, I found the muse in the undulating waters and the whispers of the wind among the trees.

The discovery of puberty in the river's pools brought me the awakening of emotions, the air impregnated with outbursts and fears, of discoveries and disenchantments. It was in those turbulent adolescent years that I began the search for consolation in poetry, a way to decipher the whirlwind of emotions that overwhelmed me and to shape the thoughts that crowded my mind. In my middle school years, during school activities, I recited the poems of Gautier Benites, a Puerto Rican famous poet and Becker, the Spain born icon poet.

My romantic loves intertwine in these pages, each verse an indelible footprint of loves found and lost, of ephemeral passions and transcendental experiences. The women who have left their mark on my sentimental life have been

7

muses and companions, sources of inspiration and causes of woes, but they have always added depth and richness to my experiences.

Retreats to nature became spiritual pilgrimages, journeys into my inner self in search of peace, serenity, and answers. In the vastness of the small woods of the neighborhood and the majesty of the hills (small mountains of lower elevation and gentler slopes), I found the clarity and renewal my spirit longed for, and in each landscape, each sunset, and each dawn, I discovered new reasons to capture my thoughts in verses.

The small 2-acre farm of my parents that welcomed me, and then the larger 32-acre farm I bought in 1983, both in my neighborhood, have been much more than just a collection of lands and nature. It has been a serene refuge, an oasis of greenery amidst the hustle and bustle of daily life. In it, I have found a space for meditation, a place where my mind calms and my thoughts find the silence necessary to unleash poetic creativity.

The trees swaying in the wind, the small spaces of fertile flatlands along the riverbanks, covered in waving grass and the gentle murmur of the river winding through the farm, have been inexhaustible sources of calm and contemplation. Every corner of this space has witnessed my deepest reflections, my woes and joys, and the muses that have whispered verses to me, seeking to capture the very essence of nature and life.

On this farm, every fold of the landscape, every nook and cranny, and every seasonal change has been an invitation to explore the emotions and sensations that lie deep within my being. Here I have found inspiration, consolation, and the materialization of my thoughts into poetry, as a tribute to the beauty and serenity that this farm has instilled in my life.

The sea and the maritime coast of my hometown, just a few minutes from the farm, has always been a center of inspiration for meditation and poetry. The sea has been the inexhaustible muse, the eternal source of inspiration. The waves crashing against the shore rocks, the salty aroma permeating the air, and the infinite horizon that fades into the distance have been silent witnesses of countless reflections, meditations, and poems that seek to capture the very essence of the sea and its eternal dance with the coast. It always reminds me of the Chilean poet Pablo Neruda in his Isla Negra. In 2006, I visited the poet's tomb in Isla Negra, Chile, to pay tribute to this icon of Latin American poetry, and I felt the mysticism of that place, which I compared to the sea of my hometown.

The sunsets and sunrises that stain the sky in golden tones have been a canvas for my thoughts and verses, in front of the sea on some bar by the water's edge, at Pico de Piedra beach, or in the seafront apartment in Carrizales, both in my hometown.

The sea has triggered a ceaseless current of emotions and thoughts when contemplating its majesty. Its imposing presence has served as a catalyst for deep meditations, inducing introspection and a search for meaning in everyday life. The tides, cyclic phenomena that reflect the eternal dance of existence, have nourished the soul by providing inexhaustible metaphors to express the cycles of life, the flow of time, and shifting emotions.

Walking along the maritime coast, with its sun-bathed beaches, collecting small seashells, has served as a backdrop to evoke the fleeting beauty of life and the persistence of humans in the face of the untamable force of the waters. In many of the verses, pulsates the influence of the sea, as a symbol of freedom, hope, melancholy, and strength, anchored in the rich history and in the everyday life of our people.

My struggles for equality and against discrimination have been fervent battles, fueled by outrage and a longing for justice. In my writings, I have aimed to build bridges, tear down barriers, and raise my voice for those whose words are ignored. Some of the poems are a cry of resistance, a call for empathy and understanding, an invitation to reflection and change.

And in some of the verses, in every line, in every stanza, beats the unconditional love for my children, the light that illuminates my path, the very reason for my existence. In them, I found inspiration, strength, and the certainty that my words, ephemeral as they may be, will leave an indelible mark on the world I will pass on to them.

These pages, filled with dreams, misfortunes, passions, and struggles, reflect life itself, an echo of the universal emotions that interweave our lives. I hope that whoever delves into these poems finds comfort, inspiration, and the certainty that, in the diversity of our experiences, we find the invisible thread that unites us all.

Some of the poems you will find follow the structure of modern sonnets, with their rhythm and cadence, while others break away from any formal style, embracing free verse and creative freedom. But each poem contains a message about the experiences, passions, and feelings experienced by me.

Each verse, each stanza, each poem represents an ode to my own life. I hope this humble collection of verses is a song to life, an echo of shared emotions, and a companion in the ups and downs of existence as a tribute to the autumn of my life. Welcome to these Odes to Life.

With affection and gratitude,

Nicolás Muñoz-Muñoz

About the Poetry Collection

The poetry collection "Odes to Life" is a journey through the experiences the author has lived. Romantic songs, his concerns for nature and philosophy intertwine in these pages, each verse an indelible mark of loves found and lost, of ephemeral passions and transcendental experiences. These pages, full of dreams, misfortunes, passions, and struggles, reflect life itself, an echo of the universal emotions that weave our lives together. Those who immerse themselves in these words will find comfort, inspiration, and the certainty that, in the diversity of our experiences, we find the invisible thread that connects us all.

Some of the poems you will find follow the structure of modern sonnets, with their rhythm and cadence, while others break away from any formal style, embracing free verse and creative freedom.

Yearned Adolescence

In youthful years, life was but a trail,
Of long paths and dusty footprints, where,
We walked free, as twin souls there ,
Feeling the world open, it's beauty and sincerity, frail.

Evenings were games of mystery's veil,
Climbing trees, our fortress lairs so rare,
Hunting guavas, star fruits beyond compare,
Juicy mangos, in the dry solstice air.

Riverside meadows, our lands of adventure.
Those sweet quenepas, like kisses, treasured,
Stolen with laughter, in the humid enclosure.
Young laughter of the mischievous tethered .

It was the path of my youthful days,
Where winds wove dreams in wonderous displays,
We wandered, souls in bloom, bare feet on tiles,
Tasting freedoms, in our world without trials.

The distant whisper of the brook's tune,
Witness to adventures and songs under the moon,
In the sturdy arms of oak trees' embrace,
I hid my sweetest emotions, a secret space.

In rebellious wheels, with schemes so clever,
Stole sugarcane, our laughter echoed forever,
And in calm rivers, we'd fish our fill.
All our treasured conquests, a thrill.

On the way to the river, fishing was our promise,
Shrimps dancing in the current,
A game of patience and skill,
A triumph tasting of dawn, in the sunlight's glance.

We were seekers of the purest spring,
A fountain springing forth like poetry to bring,
A clear mirror of a safer age, a pure reflection,
Where life and dream merged in sweet perfection.

Now, in the shadow of the ancient spring, so dear,
A pure mirror of secrets old, I hold near,
There I shelter my dreams of tomorrow,
And drink from waters that quenched my sorrow.

Those colorful years, a vivid epoch's became,
Treasures stored in my soul, in full acclaim,
Steps from a time that flies on rapid wings.
 I search the shadows for the longing it brings.

Today I return to the river, the tree, to childhood's grace,
Along paths worn by time's relentless pace.
My memories, the truest essence I can embrace,
Of that age the river took, leaving no trace.

Oh, adolescence, altar of thought so bright,
In my soul stands that eternal monument of light.
Those days I see as distant stars so grand,
Lights weighing more on my heart than planned.

Downpour

Your expressions of love are gentle showers,
that on the hot summer mornings,
refresh the heat with tender powers.
A downpour where we are yearning.

Your voice, a gentle breeze that guides,
the beating of a heart that never hides.
The eternal fire that in the soul abides,
and in every verse, for you, it confides.

Your eyes, two beacons that light
the dark night of woes outright.
Your laughter, a melody taking flight.
on paths where light pierces the night.

To a Friend

We tread paths of verdant hue,
hand in hand, with resolute stride,
your presence, refuge, and guide,
faithful companion, honor shines in you.

Together, in adventure's ardor anew,
we share the same sky as kin allied,
your friendship, a treasure does abide,
in each trial, a bond that grew.

In battles, my shield, my banner's aid ,
in laughter and tears, you stay near,
a steady pilot in seas of doubt that wade.
In each gesture, a pact of peace appears.

A beacon in the mist, my friend so dear,
together, laughter and voices unfurled,
under the sun, our souls veer.
The paths bear witness to the eternal world.

In green forest or shadowy mountain's bane,
our boots dusted from time within this weaving,
secrets and hopes, shared without strain,
amid adversity, our support, unceasing.

I find solace in your honest gaze,
your loyalty, a rock midst turbulent sea's wave.
With your support, a steadfast banner to raise,
in each trial, your friendship I do crave.

Beside you, friend, on trails and lanes combined,
we embrace the earth, sky, and the breeze,
each step a tie, a firm bind,
of endless adventures, happy tales with ease.

In the whisper of tender leaves in the air,
our friendship found its humble birth,
amid laughs and talks, joys we bare,
As our offerings to the wood and river's girth.

To Infidelity

In this shadowy night, I confess,
My tears soak the ground for the sin,
A slip, a sad echo that rings within,
My soul stained in purple of excess.

My heart tastes bitterness in regress,
For having tarnished your figure so fine,
In my chest, guilt breeds and begins to find,
I long for your forgiveness with each verse, no less.

I acknowledge the hurt caused by my misdeed,
With a faint hope for mercy to intercede,
My whole being feels deeply aggrieved.

Yearning to atone for the offense, indeed,
With actions, not just with a remorseful creed,
I seek in your heart, for love's verdict to proceed.

To My Granddaughter on Her venture into Adolescence

On the day of your thirteenth spring, so dear,
these verses flow from my heart, sincere.
Your eyes, guiding stars of a glowing sphere,
reflect sweetness shy, innocent, and clear.

Latin beauty within your visage does reside,
pride and grace in your gaze deeply implied.
With intuition, intelligence you wear with pride,
and love for you in my heart does vividly abide.

You'll grow, my child, under the scorching sun.
Your own light, in my days, the everlasting one.
Brief the moment, our enjoyment yet begun.
A fleeting sparkle, a gift from the present spun.

You're the reflection and essence of my spirit's song,
Your future a promise; my devotion to you strong.
In this long journey of my life, where you belong,
you will be, my little one, my eternal song.

To My Own Self

I met you, a long time ago,
In some arbitrary place.
Today, we're here to celebrate,
a very special moment in your life.

Friend of bohemian nights and fine wine,
modest, without delusions of grandeur,
you've reached one of your journey's stops.
That's why we're here today, that's why we toast.

You can't turn back,
but you can choose how you walk.
You can pick the stops you wish to make,
and the treasures you wish to keep.

You've always done as you please.
Guard your treasures,
your partner, your children, your siblings, your roots.
Never forget where you come from.

Don't lose what yourself had when you had nothing.
Enjoy the good moments and live deeply.

On Your Essence's Anniversary

On the golden anniversary of your essence, my love,
fifty springs in your smile gently dove,
tempered like steel under the moon, serenely cool,
in your gaze, fifty suns age, a timeless jewel.

On this day of love, I sing to you, my clear star.
To you, the vibrant soul, in your fiftieth bloom by far.
Woman of tempered strength, in you our fruit confides,
graciously celebrated by our princess, Nicole.

Our daughter feels you a heroine, with depth untold.
In your garden bloom stories of devotion bold.
And in your steps, the dance of wisdom, priceless,
Seducing even time with maternal finesse, ceaseless.

You're a devoted mother, in your embrace guidance lies,
you're the eternal bride, seductive, my constant sunrise.
Your industrious focus hums a tune wise.
Our home you adorn with love, reflected in your eyes.

Bright star in my sky, always vivid, my pride.
Woman of a thousand battles, my eternally daring bride,
work in your hands, you find never out of sight.
Let not love in routine fade into the night.

In the eternal bond of love and faith, my partner tireless,
fertile warrior, in nurture, in light, relentless.
With shared goals, our efforts intertwine, boundless.
We walk together, with strength, hope and fondness.

21

In our kitchen, extravagance is both seal and art.
Passion in every dish, in every spice, every part.
You're my honey in sweet times, in sour, my tart.
Love, in your fiftieth year, let's continue the march.

By the Shores of the Danube

Turquoise blue tints your sovereign cloak,
Danube, your stream cradles legends spoke,
beneath Hungary's watchful Parliament,
Whose feet your serene waves compliment.

Turquoise blue, Danube, before you, bows are deep,
From your waters, the poet writes, the muses leap.
Before your grandeur, the Parliament bends.
Seven towers reflected; your crystal surface sends.

In Budapest, heart of twin sisters aligned,
Your flow accompanies the watcher, Buda's hill defined,
Where the world's eyes open wide, amazed,
At the orchestra of waters and lights, silently praised.

From that hill, Buda, oh, vision yearned,
Your beauty breathes peace, wars returned.
A lookout of souls, window to destinies manifold,
where the sky and your waters meet, stories untold.

You're a vital artery, whisper of trade,
A bridge of culture, where nations and beliefs are laid,
In you resonate echoes of glorious past sacrifices,
Of heroes and villains, of peace and of crises.

You are the cradle and grave of castles raised.
On your peaceful banks, in fortresses, lives blazed.
With curves, you've been the edge of mighty empires,
Calm waters, thread sewing time and mysteries entire.

Beneath your current beats' memory, a turbulent echo.
Bronze shoes on your bank, the final breath, heavy load.
The holocaust tragedy on your shore engraved,
Yet, in your sway, renewed hope is saved.

Can't forget shoes on the shore, mourning memory.
Human darkness, the holocaust leaving its felony,
Yet, still, you hold the beauty of Europe in it's whole,
Where dreams of romance still come to unroll.

You are Europe's canvas, guardian of ancient beauties,
where romance converges in the waters you display,
a serpent, breeding life in the vineyards discoverable,
on the journey to Salzburg, revealing a life so favorable.

Like an age-old serpent, sliding subtly,
You brush vineyards, where grape holds moon tightly,
on that path to Salzburg, you magnify,
and in your waters reflect worlds, stories by and by.

I bow to you, Great Danube, river of life and tales,
Of diverse lands and the sky, you reflect with flares,
At every bend, in every wave, your course a poem,
 Written in history's book, with an author's emblem.

Danube, inspiration's source, of Europe alive.
A brave stream's song that never ceases to strive.
May you flow free, blue, and forever pure,
Danube, before you, one can only admire, sure.

Before this wonder, your flow, I stand in reverence,
Oh Danube, mirror of cultures so intense.
Captivated by the charm in every curve and wave,
Your story slides, and in every heart, it bravely paves.

Danube, source of a continent revived,
solemn and eternal river, by time sanctified.
Know this, flow of time and of alchemies,
before you, the world falls silent, and admires freely.

Under your turquoise blue, people and the past unite.
A future still sails your waters, not yet lost to night.
Your majesty knows neither beginnings nor ends,
In every forgotten bend, stories become immortal trends.

Danube, river of mirrors, where sky comes to drink,
Your legacy is poetry that time can't extinguish or shrink.
In four nations of Europe, I've found you,
And in the gleam of your waters, I've embraced you true.

Deceptive Affection

False love in masks of gala dressed,
its lies adorned with utmost care,
a heart of ice, steel-locked, confessed.
beneath its feet, truth lies bare.

It chases in the shadow's vain delights,
on golden stairways, false allure,
its icy heart rejects all pleas and sights,
deaf to humanity's fervor.

An actor on life's stage plays,
without the script of grand display,
lost in its own deceptive ways,
forgetting the enchanting lyrics' sway.

In this cold charade of living lies,
a heart is sold, essence blurs,
at the path's end, where madness tries,
solitude's harsh verdict stirs.

Just skin without souls' tender beat,
love feigned, its presence naught,
fleeting flames, their essence fleet,
fade when true passion is not sought.

Reasoned Affection

It's not that I'm falling for you,
as a matter to be scrutinized.
It's that you've planted yourself within me,
and I find, from my heart, you can't be pried.

What has become of my anger ,
the will to stand tall and strong?
What has become of my resolve,
when loving you is the only thing I long?

Let's discuss my options,
and project into the future's light,
to see if statistics hold any sway,
over the heart's relentless flight.

.

Love and Science

What's happening to me, Lord, if I'm awake?
What's happening that this experience is so intense? What,
if she's all I think about, for heaven's sake?
Does my fervor hold any reason for science?

To those Dark Eyes

In the quiet nights, my gaze goes adrift,
there, in the abyss of some dark eyes,
dark as ebony, with a drunken shift,
where old and new mysteries hide and rise.

Bright suns, youthful, vivid, intense.
Caressing springs in perpetual bloom.
Their deep black harbors a flourishing sense,
spells woven in the glance of burning gloom.

Sorcery flashes, charms weaving unseen threads,
weave in the clear space a dance of thoughts,
while the flirtatious gaze, mocking, easily sheds,
turns to an interrogating voice, at times fraught.

Tender is the cheeky curve of their tears falling.
Salt descending into an internal sea.
In their weeping, joy and suffering are calling,
liquid silver sculpting a tender uncertainty, free.

I yearn to find myself in the reflection of endless deep.
I wish to unveil the secrets held by its calm.
In the darkness, decode what I secretly keep,
to penetrate the magic that inflames, the youth balm.

Looking at them, time dissolves its barriers away,
and I, a wandering pilgrim in their vast universe,
plant my dreams under those sparkling stars' array,
where my love for her is the most immense verse.

I want to let myself be absorbed by her dreamy portals.
Cross the threshold separating the earthly from divine.
Fall into that sweet captivity, a desire now my mortal,
claiming me in its intense, opaline, enchanting my mind.

Plowing the Land

Out in the fields, plow in hand,
A soul brimming with passion,
emotions turn into verses, grand,
planting in furrows, the cultivated legion.

My old father, the faithful ally,
guiding me with wisdom of old,
as the earth opens step by step slyly,
and the seed finds its resting fold.

The scent of freshly turned dirt,
intoxicates me with its deep essence,
and the cheerful birds' chirp and flirt,
stimulate my joy and awareness.

Every furrow is a promise of life,
a reminder from nature's own device.
And I, a mere pawn, am a witness rife
To the magic that from the earth arises.

With my old man, my battle partner,
Together we shape this corner land.
And in every verse that from my soul does stir,
Is etched my love for the earth, my song so grand.

To Your Complaints

How beautiful are your complaints and scoldings,
Your unrelenting care and penetrating gaze,
Your large, deep, challenging black eyes,
And your lips crafted in grooves slightly open.

Though those complaints sting me like thorns,
your scoldings hammer me like strong winds blown,
your care is a balm in every thorn, forlorn,
and your gaze guides me through my dreamy zone.

From your eyes springs the clear light of day,
and from your lips, the sweet light of life's play.
Even if at times they chastise me in their way.

But in every complaint, in every scolding,
hides a love beyond size, infinitely unfolding,
making me love you despite your tough sway.

Oh, Mama!

From afar, you're always near,
In my mind, in my dreams, my essence dear.
Your affection, your sweetness, your calming cheer,
lost in time, inevitably sincere.

Oh, Mama! Your nights and valiant fight,
for my well-being, for my tranquil sight.
Your hard and impatient plight,
and your hidden coins in the window's light.

I miss your advice, your love so true.
Your wise guidance, when life is askew,
mapping the course, the direction towards right.

Beloved mother, always by my side,
in every step, when I need to confide.
I, always thinking of you with devotion, all my life. .

Song to Prague

In the city where whispers of history are heard low,
and the Moldau river reverently bestows,
ancient soul murmuring in its flow.
Prague wrapped you in a magical canvas it sews.

Ah, the Moldau River, silver witness grand,
of loves and sorrows under its command,
it sketches Prague's path, a notable band,
marking time, vast and ever so grand.

Women, oh goddesses, eyes with blinding bright,
Tread on cobblestones of old delight,
beautiful, proud of sweet epics alight,
muses dancing under the sky's night.

Cathedrals rise, majestic to sky's reach,
gothic, fierce guardians of nights beseech.
Baroque palaces with gardens of desires each,
kissing clouds in a lavish dance just out of reach.

In chapels and cellars of Romanesque fair,
where faithful prayers still hang in the air.
They pray to a time lost in the distance bare.
Echoes of old crusades that everywhere flare.

Modernism and cubism, brothers in arts cast,
adorn your facade with bold ideas from past.
In rebellious ways decided to last,
Stamping you as different, almost steadfast.

Palaces and gardens of baroque scene sung,
Witnesses to splendor and downfall too young,
Tales of kings and revolutions wrung,
on each balcony, in each passage rung.

Spring of Prague, a cry for freedom so near,
where cold iron clashed with dreams sincere,
where silence filled with courage clear,
and history leaped, pure and not severe.

Prague, lively and eternally bold.
Your stones speak the language of old.
Bits of history, modernity foretold.
You're the muse, shaping tales forever told.

Under your sky, a canvas of lanterns and stars.
Each night paints a portrait of what you are.
Prague, where each dusk remarks,
the magic of your eternal dance, vivid and bizarre.

City of a Hundred Spires, tips to the sky,
ethereal guards of prayer and red sunrise night.
Part of a rich fabric where dreams espy,
Golden City, where one comes to fly.

In your streets, romanticism weaves in the air.
Foamy beers toast the eternal affair.
 In every corner, lyricism's there,
to the beat of a Czech heart, tender and rare.

Your fresh brew, romance in every sip,
Joy shared and lavishly let slip,
In taverns, spirits take a trip,
Liquid poetry in my soul now sits.

Song to the Sea of My Town

By the shores of the sea that cradles my town,
I find a source of eternal delight.
Its waves, its rocks, its scent, and its sound,
the essence wrapping my piece of the sky so bright.

It's the sea of fishermen singing their song,
seeking the eternal source that calls them to swoon.
Against waves crashing the rocks in like a monsoon,
a salty aroma perfumes the air, breathing it in at noon.

Each sunset paints the sky with gold,
facing the sea's unique dance bold.
Sunsets highlight its immense fold.
A masterpiece, with enchanting stories told.

The sea, in its grandeur, leaves me in awe,
stirring tides of emotions and introspection raw.
Its cycles mirror the dance of creation's draw,
in its flow, poetry arrives with the breezes gnaw.

On the beaches, boats proudly wave,
Witnesses to the pulse of a daily life they brave.
Each scene turns into pure poetic stave,
and in every poem, the sea its beauty engraves.

Freedom, hope, melancholy, and strength.
All these hues the sea has brought to length.
More than a landscape, a rooted ancestral thread,
Beating in every stanza with a legacy widespread.

The sea of my town is an icon of beauty so bright,
A source of the deepest inspiration's light.
Its turquoise blue shines with a perfect height,
And its white sandy beach exudes a regal might.

Its waves with their foam dance with ease,
Caressing the coastline, moving at peace.
Lovers let passion take place of their tease,
As the sea breeze twirls sensing the caprice.

Oh, sea of my town, with your enchanting spree,
Captivate all with your exquisite glee.
In my poetry, you're the core of what I see,
Covering each verse in my song so free.

Song to the full Moon

Under the blanket of the starry night,
rises the silver concert of the moon so bright.
Its seductive light wraps us with delight,
in a dance of passion that dazzles in flight.

Nervously reflected in the river's stream,
the moon watches us in a silent gleam,
whispers secrets to the wind and to my dream,
accompanying the encounter with a serene beam.

In its bright, cool, and tranquil nights,
we've met, passionate in love's melodious heights,
under the spell of its tender lights,
building a love through laughter and sights.

A conspirator in our secret ventures,
guiding us in each clandestine pleasure,
whispers promise of dreamy treasures,
as together we explore new measures.

This is my hymn to the moon, my muse,
illuminating our nights with its seductive fuse.
Gifts of pure emotion it will infuse.
Oh, moon, witness of our love's true truce.

Song to Solitude by the River Shore

In vast silence, inner temple bright,
where eternal thoughts take flight,
Welcome, solitude, sweet teacher grand.
Under your wing, my spirit takes its stand.

Confidant of heights, sweet lady true.
In the flight of thought, I find you.
Beside you, pure essence's line is drawn.
In your calm, the soul is reborn.

Faithful witness of my soaring dreams,
solitary companion, it seems,
In your embrace, my living essence transcends,
in the shelter of a contemplative peace that mends.

By the murmuring river's serene edge,
where nature's lingering pledge,
I feel the sigh of clear waters' gift,
reflections and memories swift.

The cosmos' vastness contemplates me,
while life around takes shape fundamentally,
and in the river's blessed sweet song,
my silence soars, free and long.

Solitude resembling the waters' depth,
reflective, hidden realms it bequeaths.
In your mirror, truth does find,
my sincerest self in your course aligned.

You're a whisper, a spellbinding delight,
in every deep silence's memorable flight.
My soul, clear, facing with no fright.
Broken dreams and triumphs come to light.

The river, voice of pure transparency told,
evokes my highest consciousness to flow.
In its flowing, constant, and wise path,
I discover my own self; I unravel my own wrath.

Faithful silence that whispers truth,
unveiling the turbid, uncouth,
my entire being in solitary support,
among fractured dreams and inner rapport.

On the banks of my river, calm comes near,
while its song soothes my soul's sphere.
Leisurely I walk by the tranquil shore,
recalling those victories in grandeur soar.

Solitude, in deep meditation's grasp,
cradles me in its fertile clasp,
of waters pure flowing without end,
in the river mirror my own life blend.

By the crystal waters' glistening shore,
my being delves, my mind aligns more,
and in the waters' murmuring thrum,
new thoughts in my soul drum.

By my river's edge, immense silence in sway,
where the current traces time's play.
In pure flowing waters, enchantment grand,
solitude and I in tranquility stand.

Alone, but not truly by myself in rhyme,
with solitude, in peace, I shed past's grime,
In waters flowing effortlessly, timelessly divine,
I summon solitude with me in my cosmic define.

With each drop of the whispering river's stream,
the harmonious nature's peaceful theme
unveils truths in each moment's gleam,
and the voice of the soul in stillness's gleam.

The loyal whisper of the wind, a guide's due,
revealing the path, harmony so true.
In the deepest nook of my inward spree,
with solitude, I learn to renew and see.
Traversing shattered dreams afar,
and the achievements stretching in time's scar.
Examining in quiet my history's mar,
finding peace in my memory's star.

Solitude, friend of the ethereal so grand,
Fashions the inner temple, a steady band,
In the vastness of its pure breast's furl,
I discover, define, and assure my inner world.

Thus, in silence, solitude wraps its hue,
weaving a tapestry with threads anew,
stitching in silence my destiny's true,
where alone, I find my path askew.

Song to my Estate Forest

In my farm out in the wide countryside, the forest sings,
with its tall, lush trees that nature brings,
By the river that once flowed furiously in springs,
intense greenery of advancing vegetation swings.

The drizzle showers my forest with love's subtle art, Fresh
aroma imbues the air, becomes a part,
landscape of brilliance, nature's grand feat.
Nature's hues align with heart's passionate beat.

In every corner, magic delicately twines,
Each leaf whispers history through vines,
The forest shares its secrets as it pines.

In my poetry, the forest becomes my muse,
in its grooves, inspiration takes its flight,

Song to My Estate nature marvels.

In my estate, where my steps softly tread,
nature marvels and oasis in daily bustle of,
a serene haven, mirror of nature's eternal thread,
where I find peace in the paths of love.

Dancing trees, swaying to the wind's embrace,
show gratitude in every gentle trace.
Rolling meadows and hills with vigor grace,
and the river murmurs, slow in its chase.

The whispers of the river, tranquil chime,
a deep echo of timeless rhyme.
My estate, monument to stillness prime,
sketching countless hopes in my soul's climb.

Every corner holds my deepest thought,
silent voices finding echoes sought.
Invisible muses turning mud to wrought.
Life here generates fertile, creative thought.

In my estate, spontaneous poems appear,
each evening, a canvas painted clear,
sky dyed in golden hues,
each dawn filled with pages to infuse.

Under the shade of supportive, leafy trees,
I find refuge for my dreams with ease,
witnesses to my fanciful mental sprees,
inspiring verses that truly seize.

Song to a Tale of Inequality

At the corner of this forgotten street,
my voice echoes strong and clear, no retreat.
I sing for people deemed incomplete.
In every verse, a cry of valor is complete.

My roots entwine in broken chains past,
witness to merciless struggles vast.
My skin is a map of victories and losses.
Five centuries of inequality ring among the moshes.

Interlaced with chains of discrimination,
underrepresentation, the quest for liberation.
My skin a tapestry of frustrating confrontation.
Eyes reflecting centuries of freedom's negation.

Tired of gazing towards an uncertain fate,
facing a system that doesn't abate,
my verses a cry in fire for truth that's innate.
My poetry is a beacon proclaiming a clear state.

Weary of looking with blinded eyes,
battling against that colonial guise.
These verses blaze, unbridled cries,
verses of light, the truth popularize.

Each word an act of sheer resistance,
the voice of those silenced in existence.
In every verse, a new sense's insistence.
Equal rights I aim to instate acceptance.

They won't silence me, my voice remains vibrant,
I'm poetry of protest—a voice so fervent,
expressing to the world my tireless combatant.
My verses are a bridge to equality's ascent.

Confession with a Pilsner beer

In the dimness of a remote bar's counter,
rests a chilly glass, foam and droplets play,
a pilsner with me in the quiet array,
in Czech Republic's legacy, holds our encounter.

I confess to the pilsner, my essence's guard,
unveiling what I cannot shout all barred.
It listens in silence, doesn't judge too hard,
absorbs my sorrows like a subdued bard.

Bitter in its touch, like a silent farewell,
between my fingers, destiny's bell,
each sip a journey, each bubble a tale,
a lament that ascends, a desire frail.

Bitterness wrapped in golden cloak's tide,
a nectar of a god in mortal hide,
each sip a tenderness that serves,
deafened silence by love's final curves.

The meandering bitterness in your glowing flair,
echoes the soul, of dull color lines that dare.
For a muse elusive, cruel, its reign,
which takes promises, leaving only pain.

I see myself in you, in your cold, copperish gleam,
mirror of their eyes, of that piercing dream.
Bitterness in your essence, like wandering love's esteem,
like hope that flickers, then fades in the stream.

Like copper, your hues hiding secrets true,
recalling her hair in the twilight's hue,
reflection of paths old, paths no longer new.
In your amber, a place to rebirth imbue.

Each sip a chant to yearned passion's sight,
to a phantom of a woman's just borrowed light,
here with you in this bar's late-night hum,
building in each verse fortress of wax, that drum.

Oh, beloved cruel, in your ending true,
feeding the vision, emptying life's due.
My pilsner consoles in her elusive cue,
in its bitterness lies hope anew.

This pilsner rests, listens, consoles too.
Its body of hops and malt in circadian stew,
my senses' languor, my discordant song pursuing,
in its coppery luminesce, my passion renewing.

In my lips' bitter seal where it tastes,
in the froth escaping, where memories are laced.
So, I drink and confess to my most certain peer,
a bitter pilsner, my cure, my life's beer.

You, in your liquid peace, cradle me in the drift,
companion through sorrows in your mystery's lift,
I yearn for your embrace to dispel his lasting thrums,
drowning my heart in your solace, in your sums.

For every sip taken, for every bitter drop,
hope fades away as life's frame continues to lop.
To you, pilsner, I tell, in my worn-down plea.
My poetry dreams of love's distant escapee.

With every raised glass, a feeling sinks under,
Exploding in the throat's stark blunder,
oh, pilsner, my silent soliloquy's trustee,
in your bitterness, I find my sacred glee.

Make me a firm bark, like you, faithful bottle,
I wish to forget those eyes, misleadingly cajole.
Sing with me to heartbreak, to love so futile,
a passion fading, eternity's fruitless.

Every sigh I let escape tints your froth,
entwining with hops futile for comfort's prof.
With every fresh swallow, a tear goes awry,
yet in every drop remains yearning spry.

This bar witnesses my confessed verse.
In the bitter airs and barley's imberse,
hear how dreams of time now diverse,
leave with sips on this night's ceaseless hearse.

To you, golden beer, confidant of this age,
each bubble eases my burden, my rage.
With your bitterness and color my truth unfurled.
Here, my confessions in this street bar world.

Dance of the Ferns

In the spring, ferns rise tall and proud,
lush foliage, trembling fronds do not hide,
gracefully they dance in shadow's shroud.
Refuge and coolness, with the wind as guide.

In their love for shadows, in indirect light's way.
They sprout in dampness, like legends stray,
achieving their constant realm, day by day.
Their purifying essence, their world in sway.

Ferns rise in elegance, dignified as brawn,
lush, delicate, in the air they mourn,
under the shadow's dance they are drawn,
their exuberant foliage creatively born.

Lovers of dusk, in attractive light so indirect,
in the moisture, their enchanted retreat is detect.
Purifying the air, in subtleties introspect,
offering shelter to birds as their respect.

Purify the air with altruism's touch,
in twilight's veil, with seductive clutch.
Ferns crave their purifying rush,
crowning the landscape with a tranquil hush.

Where Are You, Jesus?

Jesus, King of all beauty and grandeur's call,
your justice illuminates every city's enthrall.
You promised equity for humanity, for all,
but today, your message I cannot recall.

You weren't extraordinary by what eyes did find,
but by the divine light in the deepest mind entwined,
ready to dwell in poverty, almost left behind.
A humble, simple face, your life's essence enshrined.

You surrounded yourself with common, sinning kind,
to reveal true beauty that man should unwind.
Born to peasant parents, humble souls designed,
in a modest manger, no grandeur to bind.

The peasants, your most loyal following band,
in your simplicity, purpose and truth taught.
But today, your teachings misconstrued and canned,
your love's message in the darkness can't be sought .

Where are you, Jesus? Are you still among us,
in every tender look and gesture virtuous?
In the humble and afflicted, in those muted thus?
Your legacy teaches us to love with trust.

Oh, Jesus, remain in our lives with might,
May your presence guide us with wisdom so bright. Let's
revive your message in day's pure light.
In solidarity, let's find joy, blazing and right.

Where Are You, Socrates?

Before the tribunal of excess, we inquire,
Where are you, mentor, when do your values inspire?
Knowledge as virtue, you proclaimed in the agora,
Yet today, ignorance rises as if it were an aurora.

What happened to the integrity you bequeathed?
Lost in shifting sands of appearances, it faded beneath.
You, maestro of the soul, architect of noble thoughts,
left us the compass of self, the mortal's knots.

As days elapse, elusive and fleeting,
your memory urges the just, patient, and greeting.
The quest for truth through dialogue slips away,
while your shadow, in obscurity, holds the mind at bay.

In the core of ethics, you ventured and pioneered,
the human soul, a conscious, thinking theory revered.
So why abandoned we the pursuit endeared.
Virtue, integrity, mastery veered.

Your virtue, knowledge; your lance, interrogation,
in the clash against error, your philosophy's elation.
But where to find your voice in deafening vociferation,
in this maelstrom consuming our values' foundation?

Discovering the origin of passion within our psyche,
But what of the knowledge we used to highly seek?
In a world favoring ignorance that kills in perfection,
your legacy of self-transcendence we beg for direction.

Socrates, in this lost world, we seek you earnestly,
in need of your guidance, hearts fearful indefinitely.
For in the psyche, yes, where it all began,
your teachings stand as beacons guiding everyman.

Seeking integrity in deceptive appearances,
where you remind us of essence's adherence.
You, whose example infused us with virtues pure,
we long to follow your principles, immutably sure.

We traded you for fleeting pleasure and convenience,
forgetting the soul finds solace in essence's resonance.
Wherever you are, Socrates, in reason's echo so clear,
revive the search for a life without fear.

Confident in your legacy, we row with might,
for though absent, your spirit gives us sight.
We shall unearth what your death did leave us;
An examined life, the greatest treasure to proceed us.

Free Love

Free love is pure and serene,
without fear, boundaries, or scenes,
an eternal and sweet sentiment,
without obstacles, barriers, or lament.

It's love without ties, without chains,
of passions free like the wind's gains,
hearts beating with fervor and zest,
unbounded love, pure and at rest.

Guiding us with its light like a beacon bright,
a sweet, genuine feeling, boundless in its flight.
Love without masters, passions unconfined,
a fresh wind of sweet dreams in mind.
.

The Love That Fades Away

In the shadow of my loneliness,
I weep for love that does not linger,
Silently I suffer, for love now lost.
I only longed to love you, not to be crossed.

I refuse to give up your gaze so fair,
nor surrender to love now caught in despair,
I wanted to hold on with fervent plea,
to reclaim the fire slipping away from me.

The flame that once burned now seems dim,
but I persist still, in loving you on a whim.
Yearning to revive the passion so long forgotten,
even if love comes with a wound that's trodden.

Longing to love you with a love full and pure,
without giving up on a dream that may seem obscure,
I won't relinquish, I'll stand strong and sure.

I won't let go of what I truly feel,
even when the road ahead seems surreal,
hope in me is still reasonable and real.

The new and the mature love

In the vast expanse of universe I found,
a passion that within me wound,
like the dawn embraced by the light.
A new love that blossomed bright.

On my path, the sun of a fresh new day,
in every gesture, hope grew in its way.
Like an eternal blaze deep in my core,
love springs forth in a sweet rapport.

In this passion, a new direction unfolds,
a flight in emotion, a path foretold,
where this newfound love takes flight.
Could this love be eternal, pure, and right?

Yet there's the old, cultivated love that stays,
like aged wine, through nights and days,
spreading through the calm and strife,
In the monotony of a settled life.

In habit and in symmetry found,
The soul takes solace, love profound.
But an unsettled longing I can't ignore,
a conflict between passion and the peace we adore.

This love built on a sturdy base,
yet I ache for the fire's embrace.
At the crossroads of this inner fight,
seeking redemption, a solution in sight.

I yearn for peace in this binding bond,
where new love and mature love respond,
intersecting in my need for release,
from this bleak and troubled peace.

Can one exist in this dire plight,
loving two women at once, despite?
The heart has dealt a cruel hand,
I'm lost in this confusing stand.

In the twilight of my town

In the twilight of my beloved town,
the sun in a golden hue sets down.
Its rays dancing on the tranquil sea,
in calm and serenity wrapping me.

With each sunset, a peace descends,
nostalgia fills my thoughts, it amends,
reflecting on the past I've left behind,
dreaming of a future yet to find.

On the horizon, the sun bids adieu so grand,
like a poet concluding, making his stand.
Its rays fading into the distant line,
leaving a sky of colors that intertwine.

The sunset, a moment so sublime,
your golden brilliance, a peaceful chime,
inspiring dreams with limitless grace.
These loving moments, a warm embrace.

In each dusk, I find inspiration gleaming,
in the sky's canvas, colors streaming,
my pencil dances to emotions' tune,
crafting verses under the crescent moon.

So, in the twilight of my cherished town,
the sunset remains, my muse renown.
Each verse a winged feeling's flight,
guiding me towards the faint light.

The impressive bamboo

The impressive bamboo stands strong,
reaching for the sky, in a creaking song.
It guards the ravine, resilient and grand,
dancing amidst sounds, wind in command.

With grace it sways, gentle and divine,
singing to the river in a mysterious line.
Patiently it waits for my fleeting sight,
bowing reverently, seeking peace in its light.

In the river's gorge, majestic and tall,
the bamboo challenges the sky at its call.
Dances to laughter's melodious tone,
protecting the banks in its noble zone.

Flexible to the wind, tales it portrays,
the bamboo stands, unwavering in its ways.
Nothing can break its resilient fight,
in its mystical music, dressed in delight.

In a glorious rebirth or resurrection anew,
I wish to be bamboo, strong yet true.
Defying the wind in beauty's attire,
shielding the river with roots that inspire.

Versatile bamboo, share your story's lore,
of winds and storms in your melodic dance.
Unyielding in your victorious stance,
your mystical song, refreshes the core.

Heart's Harmony with Mind

In a vibrant debate, these sides collide,
the heart and the mind, as guardians side by side.
With voices and intentions so uniquely defined,
they lead our steps on paths confined.

The heart, a poet ablaze with fervent fire,
beats to emotions, oft whim and desire.
A torrent of passion, of feelings uncontained,
in its chaos, we find ourselves pained.

The mind, contrastingly, a sage so wise,
analyzing each choice with frozen eyes.
The voice of prudence, of clear-sighted sense,
guiding us away from any consequence.

But which to heed in times of choice so prime?
Which path to choose, in this dance with time?
To live happily, wisdom does advocate,
listen to your heart, let it navigate.

In simple matters with feelings strong,
the heart should lead, right or wrong.
For in love, in passion, in every instance,
the heart holds sway, without resistance.

Yet in grand decisions, of critical accord,
where the future lies, where goals are stored,
the mind must raise its cautious voice,
advising with diligence, offering a choice.

Actions fueled by unruly emotion's flight,
may lead us to darkness, to a sorrow night.
Romantic flames may our senses ignite,
sans reason's guide, we're lost from sight.

So, in this delicate balance they uphold,
the heart and mind, a union bold.
To follow the heart in daily tunes,
mind in grand schemes, avoid misfortunes.

The Smoke of the Still

In the brew of the still, forged in homely heat,
the night guards the art of rum, sustaining sweet.
Men of earth and sugar, sweat upon their brow,
seek the altar of quiet waters, dreams to endow.

Beneath the shadow the brook used to enfold,
hidden by the dance of trees, the air's story told,
keeping secrets of the land, a sweet beating heart,
of time suspended in the well, a flowing art.

The still, a fierce sentinel on summer eves,
awakens memories of ancient dreams it weaves,
where rum, the nectar of gods, is born silently,
and the fear of discovery kindles reflexes quietly.

In shadows, an ancestral chant resounds low,
beneath the brook's veil, whispers of trees aglow. Cautious,
the moon's glow in the high sky,
watches the cane ritual as rum runs dry.

In the brook's shadows, beneath guarding palms,
hope blooms to rise from fiery qualms.
In exhausting toil and the night's elixir rare,
fear pulses weakly; louder pulses hard work there.

Sweet molasses, pure honey streams flow wide,
flavor of life, nurturing sweet labor's stride.
A scent intoxicates the skin, soul cries clear,
in memory of time, and in heart appear.

Night's labor, sky's accomplice in the dance,
to the fire's ritual, lights that enhance.
Silent witness to the whisper, the enchantment,
in my blood's story, the still's a blessing granted.

My childhood soul absorbs the dimming light,
shadow vigilant, faithful to father's sight.
Fear of light, of steps that peace may smite,
searching the ferment of ambitious might.

The still guards flavors of memory pure,
in its bubbles, tales of glory endure.
Even in the fear of uncharted shores afar,
brewing the drink under shadows' arm.

Mystery in the full whisper of the breeze,
each drop distilled, path it flees.
Simple life, inheritance of fire's serene,
among the canes, rum's anthem keen.

Framed by bamboo, by crisp spring's glee,
hiding the aged artisan's treasure and spree.
In the decade of hope, mixing fortune's play,
golden rum, perfect blend, healing ray.

Rum flowed from molasses, fermented delight,
nights accomplice of eternal insight.
A song to the sky, veiling freedom's cheer,
each drop a call to just fraternity clear.

Smoke ascends, tales in swirling flight,
of lives twined in cane and moonlight's might.
Each bubble in the still, a dream alight,
the dance continues, my purest plight.

In those nights of craft rum, mystery unfurled,
past and present where essence twirled.
In smoke, fear and hope embrace and clutch,
and in each bubble, the peasant's life we touch.

The Fisher on the Skiff

Down by the coastal shore, the fisher's call,
casts his nets with a mighty thrall.
His mate watches from the beach's side,
the sun gleams bright, its radiance wide.

Rusty platforms of old artillery stand,
silent watchers by the land.
Mutual witnesses of wars bygone,
protecting the fisher at early dawn.

The gentle sway of the waves invites,
The reflection, the calm delights.
Seagulls dance above the nets spread,
signs of a catch, on the fisher's thread.

A stool awaits to clean the day's haul,
on the golden sands where woes forestall.
The poet seeks noble emotions true,
with patience and hope, his spirit grew.

On Carrizales' golden beach I crisscross,
slow steps, carrying burdens and loss,
freeing my thoughts, in the morning's gleam,
fishing for feelings in summer's dream.

Fresh and good fish I aim to find,
yet in truth, it's dreams that I bind.
In search of inspiration, I walk my way,
admiring the fisher's workday fray.

The Rio Grande

Beneath the radiant sun in fields afar,
where greenery beams from every tree,
flows the Rio Grande, crystal stream,
passionate in its winding dream.

Among the rocky, crystal brook's bed,
its waters clear and pure are led,
like secrets whispering to the breeze,
inspiring poetry with ease.

Verdant flora in its lush embrace,
accompanies every tranquil trace,
as it runs gentle, tender, fine,
breathing life in its grand design.

Serpentine, dancing amongst the stones,
the current in grace and soft tones,
whispers melodies the heart awaits,
gifting sweet tunes to environment's fate.

There, the spring of waters pure and clear,
where life revives without a tear,
the source that nurtures this secure flow,
bringing calm to all it does bestow.

Crystal current, treasured sight,
with shimmering light, fresh and bright,
you're the lively soul of my cherished land,
forever in my verses grand.

Rio Grande of Aguada in your vibrant hue,
bathing my homeland, love anew,
your tranquil, crystalline stream so serene,
forever inspiring, in poetry's spleen.

At the Brink of the billiard

At the brink of the billiard, where the green cloth lies,
I relish the decisive stroke, where daring luck decides,
the white ball spins in its unbound dance,
amidst chalky sounds, the game takes its stance.

Feeling the soft cloth under my steady hand,
tracing geometries silently, a choreography quite grand.
Precision measured in a mundane space,
where the leading ball sets the joyous pace.

The cue between fingers, akin to an artist's brush,
the white ball whispers, the silence it will crush.
Steady pulse, gaze locked, a duel intense,
for melodies of love that the jukebox dispense.

To the rhythm of the jukebox, a tearing sound,
narratives of abandonment and past tales abound,
float upon the shots, victory's tether wound,
to the tune of weeping for the once-loved crowned.

Walking the perimeter with strategic drive,
balance as master, flexibility thrives.
The table, an altar where pulse is kept,
in this living board victory and sentence are adept.

Friendship sealed with a toast to clink,
emotional connection evokes affection's brink,
hearts intertwine like sparks of old,
the clash of balls, my fervor behold.

Reunion of old and new friends alike,
imagination awakens, creativity to spike,
hope gathers us, challenges invite,
visualizing paths, minds take flight.

In this sanctuary of colors and shapes,
the game turns theatric, poetic takes,
lines intersect, angles inform,
life as ethereal as the game's norm.

In the plot of billiards, resolution beats,
pleasure a wave that ever repeats,
solving problems, mimicked in play,
from the initial hit to the final day.

And in that sweet tension of waiting and resolve,
in the game of touch, calculation that evolves,
lies the essence, the joy to be,
a hit to sadness, an escape so free.

While music plays its comforting role,
in the spherical dance, spinning without a goal,
the pain of disappointments, for a moment lost,
the jukebox accompanies, memories crossed.

In every shot, in every move, life mimics the game,
where billiards reigns as master and learning, the flame.
So, at the edge of this table, amidst friends and cheer,
in the corners lies an escape, from fatigue so near.

Fickle lover, among cloths and woods arrayed,
of this pool hall, my green flag swayed,
a melancholic game with ballad in the air,
amid melodies, emerges the desire to forget in there.

At the edge of the cloth, world fades away,
only balls, game, and song to stay,
life simplifies, though outside reflects,
a complex universe of passion and regrets.

The Last Virgin of the Caribbean

Here the rain falls, my memories sway,
to the sea, white sands convey,
of that place where not a drop descends,
where wind blows, the shore it amends.

They name her Flamenco, timid and meek,
yet she asks you to seek,
Culebra, tender, sensuous form defined,
the last Virgin of the Caribbean, refined.

In her, I recall that moment in sight,
the sand etching your mark, bright.
Me by your side, dreaming of our lay,
of that night, the most beautiful display.

In the hour of the journey

Morning rays timidly peek,
through the windows of branches, sleek,
to light your face still in sleep's peak.
By your side, I'll be, if me you seek.

It's time to embark on the path we know.
Through autumn's dressed lane, I go,
up the hill, face forward, into the glow.
My footprints with you, like in the snow.

I'll cross the thin silk screen that divides,
this life from eternity's wide tides,
on a day or night, when fate decides.
Yet in the city with you, my spirit resides.

After seeing me cross that border line,
alone, you'll continue the path of shine.
But in every spring, my echo will be your sign.
From eternity, I will be with you, oh partner of mine.

The Beauty Within

In this world, where judgment comes so quick and near,
they ask me with disdain, not even blinking, hear,
"That woman, so plain, what in her face appears?"
But it's her essence, her aura, and dear.

Blinded by her light, they fail to really see,
her kindness, character, the essence of my glee.
With laughter, she dissolves pain naturally,
her sharp wit, a wake-up call spiritually.

Her humor's a beacon in the densest fog's embrace,
a sunbeam in my soul, bringing life and grace.
She's the most beautiful sequence in my life's trace,
turning dull days into treasured space.

She's a serene landscape where I find lasting peace,
an artwork for the soul, never seeking to deceive.
Her brilliance is a fire that will never cease.
Intellectual spark that in me won't release.

Blinds are those who only see the outward shell,
Unable to appreciate Eden from her well.
Her inner beauty, the deepest part that swells.
It's what I admire, makes her mine, as time tells.

She's my guiding light, in all that's seen and unseen,
for all she gives so freely, incalculably, serene.
More than just a face, she's an indescribable scene,
my muse, my peace, my inspiration, in between.

So, when asked why I hold such a deep respect,
I'll answer truthfully, with no hint of neglect:
"It's her being, everything that now connects,
and in her 'imperfections,' my heart reflects."

And if they question the love that I present,
I'll smile, for she's my every cent.
In her intellectual world, inspiration is lent.
Her soul, her essence, my most beautiful descent.

Lighthouse

Your constancy is like a lighthouse, bright.
Always there, in darkness or light.
A sacred symbol of safety, ever so bold.
Always there, your story told.

You mark the shore's inviting embrace,
from the sea's shadowed space,
through dark nights and narrow ways.
Always there, guiding our days.

In my trials, you're both my helm and anchor,
Always there, my steadfast flanker.

Today I want to Merge with You

On an ordinary day, many years past,
while scratching my heart,
seeking relief from a romance rash,
I unearthed a strong thread of love for you at last.

I kept you waiting, a silent plea.
But today, I want to merge with you, let it be,
in an eternal love,
that walks with me beyond this day, above.

From this love, a daughter will bloom,
A witness to my love, in the eventual gloom.
If, as life's laws do propose,
Should I depart before you, she'll be the rose.

Equal Among Equals

In the grand cradle woven of stars above,
the founders' dream stands strong and true,
hoping equality befalls every soul with love,
for every soul in the standing Nation that grew.

The battles of time, not forgotten, stay,
in each heart with equal fervor does sway,
like the enchanted bell's echoing sound,
calling to all, excluding no one around.

Political vigil, a burning star in the night,
rights for which daily battles are fought.
Justice that democracy craves with all its might,
to be equal among equals, not as the tide brought.

The people will wake from their slumber deep,
their clamor for equality openly weep.
In their voice and strength, they'll finally see,
self-determination, a rightful decree.

Let not, Nation, your foundations delay,
under the broad blue of your flag's sway,
may each of your children see the same day.
Equality be the light, the foremost way.

In the cradle of a foundational dream,
under banners of freedom that brightly gleam,
in every law and fraternal scheme,
an ideal of equality was the supreme theme.

On the canvas of sisterly stars, so bright,
echoes the sound of many a fight,
claiming equality in every sight,
of those fighting for democracy's light.

Yet, there remains a deficit in rights given,
parity in votes, still unforgiven.
A people in their struggles not driven away,
striving to keep this dream from being riven.

At the dawn of justice, hopeful and bright,
self-determination raises its banner high.
Other nations cast their gaze upon the sight,
"Equal among equals" - the noble art that lies.

People awaken from their prolonged dream,
demanding the voice that's theirs by right,
Statehood cries in their stolen beam,
and equality shines forth in their chest bright.

Let there be no chasms in rights anymore,
nor in their voices, the echo of oppression sore.
Seek parity among peers on the same shore,
children of the star-spangled core.

Politics that lift us all to the summit, fair,
with steadfast steps and destiny in hand,
the people see in the dawn's light that dare.
Self-determination is a human right so grand.

Long has been the slumber, but now awake,
the voice of the people, it's their time they stake.
Let equality no longer be forsaken,
claiming one more star in the heavens to partake.

Gardener of Dreams

In his mind, the gardener weaves a garden scene,
where dreams blossom, endlessly keen.
A gardener, mad with visions so bright,
cultivating desires in the dimmest light.

He dreams of freedom, unbound, without fear,
where romantic love soars, with no wheel to steer .
Among erotic passions and fiery quests,
his strong roots find enveloping zest.

Escapes in the rhythm of a tropical tune,
where passions rage, like a monsoon.
Love fleeting as flowers in spring's embrace.
In his garden of dreams, absence finds no place.

The gardener of dreams, with no regret in his heart,
sows the seeds of desires, where suffering is not a part.
In his poetry, his madness, and desires flow,
the gardener of dreams lets his sparklers glow.

Exploring the bounds of his imagination's terrain,
shattering the rules with each inspired strain.
Dwelling in the illusion of realms unreal,
where dreams stand temporary yet conceal.

Catharsis of a New Dawn

Among clouds of white silk, dances the dawn's light,
glowing softly, unfolding through the night.
while various birds sing at daybreak's call.
Notes of a new day rise, enchanting all.

Rumba of life, of freshness and hope anew,
emerges in every being and endeavor we pursue.
Joy resounds, new dances bloom in the air.
Life's rhythms in glory, beyond compare.

Rhythms of joy, plans that start to grow,
as the sun ascends slowly, a gentle glow.
The planet awakens, the stars take their leave,
the morning brings a mantle, set to conceive.

Life flourishes with hope and freshness once more,
each being advances with eagerness at its core.
Joy resonates, plans begin to take shape.
Life's rhythms awaken, in harmony they wake.

In the Glass of Aged Wine

In the glass of aged wine, there's peace to find,
a sense of relaxation, well-being of every kind,
smoothness on the palate, a velvet touch,
pleasurable aromas, sweet joy as such.

With good company, the wine becomes a treasure,
tension drowns, replaced by laughter without measure,
thoughts flourish, strong and sincere,
and for a moment, forgotten is every tear.

Inspiration that intoxicates the heart,
serenading a beloved, a passionate start,
under the influence of this blessed art.

With each sip, a new song plays part.
The wine's bouquet, in all its glory, all it's grandeur.
In the glass, we find redemption's chart.

The Exotic Salzburg

In the heart of a Europe that breathes,
where the Alps caress the sky in stone fingers with ease,
the Salzach is born, meandering and a calm performance,
flowing through Salzburg, with grand importance.

In this life-source river, where waters flow true,
born marked by mountains, covered in morning dew,
Salzburg, exotic, awakens at dawn's hue.
Twelve centuries in its streets, in eternal review.

Here Salzburg, the lush hilltops cry,
where "The Sound of Music" danced its joy high,
and notes still tremble in every corner of the city's scene,
in the salt that outlines the taste of its daily routine.

You sit, elegant, on your throne of ranges,
centuries embroidered on streets, exchanges.
Jewel of Europe, weave tales of war's estranges,
a tapestry of epochs, of life, it embraces and engages.

Where Mozart to the universe melodies bestowed,
where every stone and corner his genius echoed.
Music floats in the air, at every dawn's glow,
As if the heavens themselves decided to bow low.

Hidden white wealth, under emerald ground,
salt from deep mines that the city surrounds.
Through the ages, this treasure flowed and was found.
Like Jewels in the waters, by Sal Zach it's bound.

Turquoise blue their streams, from the peaks descend,
salt from ancient stories, in their waters blend.
The Alps, still witnesses, of their city's trend,
silent guardians of salt, and of brilliance they tend.

Culture finely woven in the heart of the city,
the old and the new in an embrace, so pretty.
Masterful architecture, nature's lover,
view a painting, corners vibrant, many to be uncovered.

In Salzburg, life and art in dance revolve,
traditions intertwine, modern lights solve.
Its squares, its markets, stories they involve,
In every corner, the centuries, your heart resolves.

Salzburg, alpine jewel, with your salt and your tale,
mirror of greatness, a memory's trail.
A toast with your clear water, to your legacy's sail.
In your streets, under stars, all finds its scale.

Tradition mingles with modern beats,
in cobblestone alleys, history repeats,
and in the markets, among aromas and tender treats,
a culture pulses that every corner greets.

Tradition and avant-garde, in a waltz they sway,
in the market the salt, legacy of white crystals plays,
wealth in your soil and story, close they lay,
crossing ages like rivers, immortal fray.

Oh, Salzburg, exotic pearl, a temple of contrast,
where the night embraces with lights of theater cast,
and wakes with the dawn, vast, to say,
in verses, in poetry, the vibrant life I chase, every day.

The Cherry Blossom

A mantle of friendship between sister nations.
The Tidal Basin, mirror of light under heavens, elations,
adorned with petals that Japan scatters in celebrations.
A gentle gesture, a path of peace, and deep aspirations.

There, the Jefferson Memorial stands, a vigilant witness,
contrasting the softness of the flowers in their fittest,
sculpting in time and soul a narrative, blessed:
Constant rebirth, verses in whiteness, undressed.

Their lives, subtly fleeting, dance in the air,
a backdrop of stone and memories, a contrast rare.
Their poetry under Lincoln's gaze rests there,
and essence, a step in the continual flair.

The Washington Monument in the scene does appear,
each flower seems to float, like stars so dear,
twilight's lights paint a Bohemian sky, clear,
the city is flooded with a spell of harmony for all to hear.

It's the sweet taste of spring, dissolving,
camaraderie of falling petals, peace evolving,
with each flower, a memory in the heart involving,
a lasting charm that to the soul is solving.

Washington DC's cherry trees, this brief grandeur,
paint the city in hues of a dawning allure,
where each flower weaves a story of kinship pure,
and I become a lover, in delight, secure.

The Lonely Flower

In a desolate plot, a violet flower has sprung,
uncared for, in shadows, utterly unsung,
its freshness has defied the hands of time,
in solitude, it stands, hopeful and sublime.

No one looks its way, nor does freshwater show grace,
solitary, on the brink of death's slow embrace,
until a wandering soul, without malice in space,
offers it a breath, turning its fate with a trace.

A roaming dog, gardener of misfortune's dew,
urine upon its pale petals, oddly, it bestrews,
And thus, what seemed the end, took a turn anew.

Come dawn next, my gaze meets and admires,
that violet sprout, brave, which never tires.
¡Oh flower, in your struggle, life itself inspires¡

Lips Carved in Grooves

In the silent embrace of the darkened night,
lies the smile of a silvery starry light.
Carved lips, crimson in their pure attire,
safeguard the mysteries of a tender desire.

Lips carved in grooves of fertile earth, enriched,
etched in a daring, vibrant scarlet that paints graciously
an altar, a prelude to a kept smile's stitch,
where springs slide in voraciously.

Soft lips, fields of blooming red roses to see,
youthful like April, when whispers of glee,
painted in scarlet like the sunset's spree,
holding the secret of a murmuring plea.

A gentle curve of a smile blossoming in pink,
a suggestive grin that dares and does not shrink,
juicy pathways merging in laughter, red tint,
rivers of feelings in grooves where passion's link.

A flirtatious smile, like a fleeting starry night,
emerges on those lips with a gleam so bright,
as soft and suggestive, in tranquility's light,
laughs emerge, with pearls buried deep in sight.

Tender is their touch, as the wind carries them light, playful
their gesture, in breezes that take flight,
between the folds of their charm, a feeling so right,
of a promise of love, of genuine delight.

The grooves that adorn those divine lips.
A masterpiece of an emotional trick.
Every line written in scarlet tints, a destination,
on a map of sighs, in an immortal elation.

How desire pushes me to taste their charm,
to lose myself in those crafted lips so grand.
A sweet journey captivated in a holy stand.
Every kiss is a pledge, every touch a wondrous land.

I yearn to lose myself in the silk of their spell,
in those lips carved by desire's magic swell,
to let the touch of that crimson hue, dwell,
in their enchantment not being able to is my hell.

To entangle in the magic those inviting lips, I yield,
in the caress of the enchantment their smiles I feel
to find in their gentle contours an endless field,
and in their mouth, a brush for the moon to wield.

Thus, each kiss I long for in silent dismay,
is a mere touch of two souls in a cosmic play.
An ethereal dance, my feelings convey.
Vines of passion in their magic sway.

May the meeting of those lips be an endless ride,
where each grove tells tales of old, times gone by,
and, in unison, with a kindred heart's stride,
we submerge in a sea that is infinitely wide.

A ritual of passions, their lips in singular sway,
each kiss a vow, each sigh a garden astray,
sow eternities, wrap the soul in tearful bay,
and in her mouth, be I poet, sin, lust, all, in endless day.

The Ebony Maiden

In a world where ink and light embrace,
emerges she, a young star in grace,
her steps release verses in rhythmic dance.
Concert of charm, igniting a hopeful trance.

In ebony landscapes, her slender figure sways,
a poem of curves 'neath the sun's lively blaze.
Locks of night's silky strands extend free,
in day's warmth, igniting lights to see.

Those ebony curls, wild and long they flow,
like rivers in a nightly glow.
Eyes large, deep with magic's heed,
gazes igniting dreams, fading age's need.

With her, erotic desire's draped in poetry's art,
a fervent, intense passion in the heart.
A stealthy gaze, a revealed enigma, a start,
of nights of passion, in her arms, fantasy's part.

With lips of crimson red, tempting sin's delight,
to a journey desired, there's no return tonight.
Incarnation of night, day's promise so bright,
her essence inspiring the sweetest poetry's flight.

Intelligent, her smile a loaded device,
with mischief held in her red lips, precise,
she appears as a dream muse so divine.
In her presence, my heart does pine.

Not just a body, but a fiery soul aglow,
a perfect lover, yet more, a life prized so.
With every step, defies gazes others throw,
In her, every street finds a release to show.

On her skin, tales of endless nights reside.
Each furtive glance, a promise of treasure,
where passionate love blooms without measure,
and in her embrace, all wounds can hide.

She walks free, proud, powerful, paving her way,
a queen in her realm, her gaze a universal doorway,
where secrets morph to melody's tune.
She, the muse, the poetry, night, and noon.

She, a challenge to this oft forgetful world twirl,
beauty wreathed in mystery, a beautiful pearl.
She, representation of all fantasies unfurled,
an ode to life, in its dearest swirl.

Let verses flow like the river's run,
celebrating this woman, under the sun.
May she keep walking, standout in the crowd,
with her charm and her tale, in love's shroud.

May her footsteps eternal, her laughter immortalizes.
In the memory of ages, a love that it prizes.
Girl of light and shadow, of passion and reason,
her essence is a poem, purest musical season.

The Heliconias

On the serene spring's edge in flight,
where the green forest lays its sight,
Heliconias rise, enchanting the view,
in their splendor, recalling times anew.

From Greek mount, home of divine muses,
they carry grace of ethereal art's cruises,
in colors of red, green, and gold array,
evoking the tropics, warm and gay.

Symbolizing youth, grace, and zeal's flame,
like eternal muses in their frame,
beneath the Caribbean sky, pleasing and true.

Like birds of paradise in the wind's embrace,
their parrot-like beaks, breathing grace,
the heliconias bloom, vibrant in hue.

The Youth of Yore

Those years of youthful lore,
mischievous adventures, loves, and loyalty swore,
adolescent dreams, profound and pure,
exploring the margins of freedom's allure.

Nervous escapades into unknown lands, to be seeing,
the heart beating with fervor, an intense feeling,
seeking adventures beyond earthly bounds.
Craving the enchantment happiness surrounds.

In youth, life unfolds like a canvas white.
Each step unknown if it's right.
An uncertain destiny awaiting in sight,
a vast unknown realm, both darkness and light.

Oh, youth, so fleeting and fair,
soul brimming with dreams in the air.
With every vision, hope's tender care,
open to the world, with eager stare.

The Royal Palm

In my land, the green from the palms beam,,
One stands royal, tall, and esteemed.
Under the Caribbean sun, its presence gleams,
the royal palm, in elegance, it redeems.

More than an adornment of living earth,
it stands tall, with regal worth.
with its green branches reaching high,
unfolds the beauty of its skyward tie.

Nearly a century and more, its life spans,
sweet haven for birds, shade, hope grand.
It holds up the sky, its canopy dances,
may its song endure, against winds' advances!

Its venerable presence, emblem of the land,
a serene symbol, in its green band.
Royal palm, fountain of life, pride in its stand,
in my homeland, in my farm, ever at hand.

In its majestic height, touching the sky,
in its shade, a haven, where we all lie.
Its virtues shining bright, a guardian true,
a poem of nature in each branch's view.

The Latina Princess

In the Caribbean land, 'neath the scorching light,
a Latina princess, so bold, so bright.
Her walk so sweet, her grace profound,
her gaze captivating, smile unbound.

Bronzed and slender, curves divine,
her curly locks in heavenly twine.
Smiling and passionate in every way,
with a walk so steady, claiming her sway.

Beautiful maiden, with a sculpted frame,
radiant brunette, a celestial flame.
Slender and graceful, with curves galore,
dancing leisurely, I cannot control my thoughts more.

Elusive, evasive, like the sea's swift breeze,
desired, longing, like a shooting star we see
Passionate in gestures, melodious in her dance,
latina princess, grant me some hope perchance.

Her long curls dancing in their lively spree,
radiant smile, gallant gestures she receives .
Passionate, alluring, heat's lovely amour,
elusive, evasive, love's very own lure.

Thus is the princess in her enchanted glade,
where all is possible, where none is forbade.
A beauty of land and sea, so grand,
the Latina princess, worthy to withstand.

Her voluptuous hips move to the beat,
her long, curly hair waves so neat.
Like waves dancing under starlit sky,
she brightens streets with her rhythm in the night.

Yearned for by many, she stays elusive,
impenetrable, lofty, captivating exclusive.
With a gaze imposing, unbreakable,
the Latina princess, unmatched, capable.

Her music the rhythm of her vibrant life,
in each step, in every shared laugh.
A Latina princess, of fire and calm,
passion in her essence, in her very palm.

Mysterious, like the dark of night,
her captivating beauty, her spirit lights.
Mysterious, beneath the starry above,
the Latina princess, the dreamed-of love.

The Twilight of Forbidden Love

In the twilight of forbidden love's veiled light, temptation
rises gently, a specter bright.
In hidden, excessive passions that fight,
desire unfolds in a senseless plight.

A foreign love, a flame shared in two,
burning in hearts, passion's construe.
The enveloping passion, burned without a clue,
in shadows, transgressed, nobody could see through.

In verses of forbidden love's chained plight,
voices of lament entwine in night.
The irrational attraction takes flight,
a fire burning within, a hidden light.

Forbidden love like a hidden bloom,
awakening desires, embracing gloom.
Frustration from desire, impending sense of doom,
knowing the wrong path leads to an empty room.

Desire envelops us in its concealing hold,
a battle between reason and a feeling so bold.
Reason screams with sensibility, so cold,
while the heart murmurs in its rhythmic truth to be told.

Yet guilt looms, unrelenting in its stand,
internal struggle, reason versus heart's command,
dragging us into irrational lands.

Reason confused in the ineffable tension,
the promise tying us to a binding convention,
breaking the heart with emotional detention.

The Little Old House

In the little old house my parents claimed,
echoes of youth and light remain untamed.
Fruit of collective labor's honest fame,
Memories that evoke gratitude's proclaim.

Built with hard work and pure affection,
a testament to patience and steadfast connection,
in its modest frame, without defection,
reside memories with reverence's projection.

When electric light first found its way,
illuminating walls that once looked gray.
The rooster's concert at break of day,
 melodies in perfect catchy array.

Chickens, goats, pigs, stirring sounds,
chants of rural life, dreamy bounds,
the tree, witness to nightly rounds,
aromas of coffee in kitchen, fondness surrounds.

In the little old house, my parents' care.
Memories cherished with greatest flair,
fruits of labor, love beyond compare.
The home where eternal dreams stay there.

In the little old house my parents' cherished stay,
lies the essence of my very way,
foundation of love, bonds with my kin convey.
Sanctuary for the elders, their sway.

Encounters, studies, and nearness bound,
the little old house, my soul's holy ground,
sweet corner of pure longing found.

Days of laughter, days of sorrow matched,
each corner teaching a lesson hatched,
the little old house, sacredly dispatched.

The Innocence Unbound

On the threshold of lost virginity's rite,
lie the loves of my youthful nights,
a burning heart seeking what's right,
a girl devoted, melting in love's sight.

Dreams of shared passion, hearts open wide,
Innocence's purity in full stride.
Total surrender, gratitude's gentle slide,
silent pleas through the night's tide.

Emotions blend, desire, fear, and glee,
nervous innocence, a new identity,
Excitement, surprise, curiosity set free,
anxiety, challenge, heart's temerity.

Oh, that young love, so pure, so bright,
shedding one's self in act of faith under the moon's light,
merged in warmth, in an embrace so tight.

Whispers and moans, tears drunk deep,
passion, devotion, madness, love's leap,
on the threshold of lost virginity's sweet keep.

April Lips

Lips with grooves so neatly carved,
for April's blooms they've been starred.
How lovely when those lips' part,
with ivory backdrops, a gentle start.

The Mahoganies

From deep within my estate, a voice cries.
The mahogany, in its transient note lies.
Symphony of life in its wood, implies,
with alkaloids, a path of stars arises.

Roots, subterranean fortress stark,
vascular life, power, dreams spark.
And its echo in my forest, like a bell,
Resounds, a battle against its own dark.

Red and purple, its noble cloak,
the color of royalty, in history it's bespoke.
In furniture and decks, forever afloat,
mahogany rises, in a staunch mope.

Leaf and root, in the forest's length,
offer endlessly their ancestral strength.
Yet despite its essence, strength at its calm,
the earth has wept for its lost realm.

The forest weeps, its skin engraved,
by the cowardly axe, destruction raved.
Its greatness dwindling, its nobility slave.
Mahogany, a giant, the Earth's grave.

Man, blinded by his voracious quest,
ignorant, aiding in his own unrest.
In sorrow, mahogany calls for justice's zest,
with each strike, my soul does protest.

In its rings, tales of better times,
where it thrived, free of old-time chimes.
My tribute to what's depleting, each rhyme.
Noble mahogany, in your honor, it's prime.

The Hearts that Brushed My Soul

The loves that have touched my life,
scars on my heart carefully engraved.
Each one, an echo in my being, a deep strife,
together forming a universe of stars that are saved.

Beautiful experiences that left a mark in me,
an unmistakable echo that reveals in my soul.
Their presence pulses, in my memory gleams free,
weaving my verses, my emotions as a whole.

Winged love or fleeting admiration.
Each a muse and companion in my wanderings,
etched in my being, in the light of my devotion,
sources of unrest and whispers of hopeful strivings.

In this collection of rooted illusions,
in my journey, sail stars of loves I've missed,
each one present in my parchment of gentle songs,
each woman left her steps and imprints exist.

In their eyes, I found the gleam of dawn's light,
and in their laughter, the gentle breezes whir.
Every caress, a poem in my memory bright,
and each farewell, in memory, a note so sure.

Symphony of memories, unforgettable notes,
intertwined tales, unbreakable as ropes.
Loves enduring through unchangeable forms,
golden scars, priceless in all scopes.

Each unfolded their wings in my sky's lair,
whispering tales, igniting desires with care,
Every touch, a verse written on my skin fair,
and every goodbye, a melody echoing rare.

Free to choose

At the high peak of human thought's golden gleam,
freedom to choose stands as the sovereign stream.
Choice is the key to doors awaiting release,
vast green fields await those who bestow peace.

It's the divine right to make mistakes or get it right,
to steer one's life, to be dumb sometimes and be bright.
Freedom of choice, eternal friend so dear,
invites us to the dance of life, to steer.

Our growth is in this value deeply rooted,
each step we take, our will is attributed.
Freedom, crucible of dreams and identity's mark,
in the forge of action, it sets its spark.

That freedom nurturing growth's fine bloom,
where every soul chooses in wisdom's room.
It's the chisel sculpting fate's grand statue,
in destiny's stone, free from death's venue.

Not only for happiness to find its way too,
but to better shine in society's view.
It's a foundation, a pillar of our own deeds,
the base on which we build to succeed.

In the market's ship, prosperity's sail to steer.
Freedom is the wind that makes paths clear.
Free nations sail toward greater ease and bliss,
with hope, life, and a future loving kiss.

Yes, freedom to choose, emancipation bright.
Nations thrive where choices take flight,
like a tireless beacon, guiding all askance,
freedom to choose, eternal hope's dance.

In the world's grand stage, she takes the lead,
economic freedom, a vital spring indeed.
In the rivers of the free market's clear stream,
prosperity and wealth find their dream.

My nieces and nephews

With an open heart, I raise this rhyme in grace,
singing of my nieces and nephews, warm embrace.
Though not my own, in my heart they're spun,
my blood, partners in accomplices, friends as one.

They are mischief-makers of laughter and glee,
bringing adventures that light up our spree.
Watching them grow, brief as a fleeting gleam,
like infinite time in a celestial dream.

My patience tested at each encounter's sight.
Yet their beauty is a treasure shining bright.
They are precious gems, beyond measure's toll,
a divine gift, gracious, unforgettable soul.

Though not born of my flesh and bone,
I love them immeasurably, as if my own .
They are blood and spirit, my little suns,
my allies and friends in countless runs.

The pleasure of their presence, beyond compare,
a sunbeam on days grim and unfair.
The love I hold, pure and unreserved,
an eternal bond, undeterred.

They fill my life with love and sweet delight,
every giggle and mischief, pure and right.
In their eyes, a world of hopeful chances,
a promising future in their innocent glances.

With them by my side, sorrows seem light.
Their presence in my life shines so bright.
Watching them grow, a gift from above,
a long moment, the most beautiful love.

They'll grow strong, brave, I have no doubt,
chasing dreams, challenges they'll scout.
In them, I find a blessed connection,
a divine gift, an endless affection.

Radiant Full moon

Beneath the starry cloak, full moon so bright,
you gleam in the sky, radiant in light,
witness to my longings in the dark,
a source of energy, a guiding spark.

Symbol of divinity in the night's grace,
guide for lovers in an affectionate embrace,
mistress of the sun, with gentle sway,
illuminating the path in my dismay.

Tears flow endlessly for my lost love,
awake even now, in night's alcove,
she remains silent, no solace found,
her silence - evidence of love unbound.

Full moon, a diamond in my sky's domain,
lighting my path with celestial mane,
lead me to love afar in the night's choir,
beneath your glow, in this night of fire.

Spring, tranquil haven of my dreams.

In the corridor of a fertile barren lane,
where the hill to the spring does give its gain,
emerges the crystal, ensuring fruitful diet,
tearing apart the veil of eternal quiet .

In a corner where life springs its flow,
rests the spring, source of life's glow,
its waters clear, pure, a promised sight,
refreshing the thirsty with might.

From hidden veins pure water does spring,
a gift from the earth, sky's pruning,
it flows in a constant, sweet tune,
giving life to the shores as a boon.

Birthed from the bosom of the wandering hill,
after a long journey through the dark drill,
nature destines its flow,
to be the constant liquid muse to know.

From the rocks, in a mysterious hum,
life laughs in each clear drop's sum,
and in its path it fosters so much,
greenery by its shores untouched.

The spring, a memory of emotions seen,
oasis of memories, songs in between,
source of life, a constant ally,
with its brilliant silver thread hard to come by.

Days spent with gourd in hand,
collecting the fruit, liquid grand,
treasure of the earth, by far,
hidden gift, from the subsurface star.

That stream, master of mysteries near,
heard the sincerest secrets clear,
shores in whispers, confessions shared,
held my childhood's passions with care.

Under the sun, gathering by its side,
fresh water for the day's wide stride,
silent companion of the trail I'd went,
and to the student whom school expects.

Stones of the bow, witnesses of the past,
they wielded my childhood's cast,
steps to school, innocence so vast,
the coolness on the tongue, first and last.

With each sip, a verse unspun,
the story of my life, quiet and fun,
childhood thirsty in age-old hike,
finding in you its source, dreamlike.

Playful laughs in summer's joyful days,
meetings under the starry sky's blaze,
first touches, dreams shared like a flare,
at the beloved spring, sweet and fair.

With each drop, a wish forged anew,
there, by its side, in times sped through,
we drank life in a sweet sip's cue,
weaving in each sip we learn what's untrue.

Thus flowed the spring, wise and mild,
mirror of years and fate compiled,
in its stream, a worldly sigh,
binding hearts with its melodic cry.

So, the spring, with voice so still,
tells in its murmur the story's fill,
and in its eternal flow, without delays will,
unite the days, joy with skill.

Memories now fill my silent mind,
of those days with you enshrined.
You are the spring, in time's gentle sway,
haven of my dreams, my breath in display.

I enjoy those nights.

I enjoy those nights so sweet and warm,
where in dreams, with tenderness I swarm,
and I adore your innocence and blush so true,
when exploring your body, bare to view.

I relish your gentle reproaches that arise,
as softly, your eyelids close by and by,
your form opens to my whisper's modest sighs,
and your lips press tight in surprise.

I delight in moments of passion's tight clutch,
in ecstasy, sobbing, with your breath they touch,
then I believe you're mine in dream's view,
and awake thinking you love me too.

Urgent message

It's urgent, my need to create an altar at your feet,
for the wondrous gift of being my heart's beat.
Urgent is to express my love so bold,
with all the depth my heart can hold.

Urgent is to savor your love sip by sip,
day by day, minute with no skip.
Urgent to ask how your day goes by,
what you'll eat tonight, in tribute so high.

Urgent to see your lips, chapped and dry,
etched by the lack of a kiss I can supply.
Urgent to pull you close in my solitude,
against my chest, a comforting attitude.

Urgent to journey with you away,
to the places we've dreamed, come what may.
Unable to go, time slips through my grasp,
devoted to tasks that torment and rasp.

Urgent to plead, marry me in trust,
let bindings break, rigid and just,
so societal chains no longer prevail,
let moral codes unfurl and pale.

Urgent to wake beside you each day,
in my bed, or yours, come what may,
watching the first rays of the sunshine bold,
through the window, a sight to behold.

Urgent to feel your warmth so true,
not letting time pass, our love to renew.
Do what's urgent each day just right,
loving you fiercely, with all my might.

My cigar and I

My cigar, faithful companion so kind,
an escape from life, a gentle ritual defined,
a necessary break on some hard days,
smoke rising, like dew's early haze.

The taste of tobacco sliding in my tongue,
aromatic smoke wrapping me as one,
pleasure seizing, eager to enjoy,
this fiery passion that joy does deploy.

Smoke rises, in vanishing spirals aloft,
carrying my cluttered thoughts off.
Releasing dreams, hope's reborn anew,
with each puff, a path comes into view.

Oh, the pleasure my cigar bestows,
in each draw, liberation flows.
The cigar, a symbol of days long past,
of yearnings gone, nostalgia cast.

The relaxation felt, deep and serene,
a psychological impact, thoughts keen.
An oasis in chaos, respite from the task,
no matter the fleeting moment's mask.

In life's battle, when it gets tough to bear,
I light my cigar, facing the despair,
but in the balance of pleasure and sanity,
I reach out my hand, bidding adieu with clarity.

Though harmony in your essence I find,
true peace is in a life without the wind,
My cigar, a chapter closing its book,
a farewell, goodbye without scorn, just a final look.

My Lone Star

Puerto Rico, my lone shining star,
garden of blues and greens afar,
where the sun, painter extraordinaire,
draws golden hues at dawn, colors rare.

Mountains reaching for the sky with power,
green steps, chants from heights that tower,
waves whispering in a celestial shore,
on dreamy beaches, sand, and treasure's lore.

Verdant mogotes, time's guardians tall,
flavors of limestone in wind's call,
witnesses of history and deep sentiment,
blend in the purest element.

Women of fire, skin of cinnamon hue,
queens of the universe, beauty pure and true.
Their eyes speak of divine passions untamed,
strong, serene, radiant light unchained.

Music vibrates, happiness unbound,
each corner echoing a rhythmic sound.
Merry the guitar, clave's resounding tune,
the island dances under the bright moon.

Coquí, small frog, hear it's song in the starry night,
music floating, never a tired thing in sight,
rhythms echoing at dawn's first light,
in a dance of notes, passion takes flight.

In your dishes a feast, flavors we adore,
adobo, sofrito, a taste that's never ignored,
plates telling tales of homes and hearts dear,
food that embraces, without compare, cleared.

People with open hearts, their smiles sincere,
where happiness waves as their flag near,
even in the storm, hope lingers here,
for the Boricua soul knows no fear.

Far from your shores, nostalgia blooms,
my Puerto Rico, in memory it looms.
Far from you, my heart just longs,
to return to your embrace, be where it belongs.

When the plane is landing, not to depart,
the applause is real, touching each heart.
Proud and strong, that noble feeling,
landing and the Boricua accent hearing.

I miss you, oh homeland, as I go afar,
feeling that I leave a piece of who we are,
each return is like a fresh new start,
in your arms, homeland, I wish to never part.

Constant struggles for equality's call,
your people dream of freedom for all.
Brave Islands with ideals so grand,
your feats resound, endless they expand.

Equality is your fight, noble and true,
uniting hearts with strength anew,
a voice that rises, steady and bold,
the right to be equal, in every fold.

Puerto Rico, my land, my sky, my tide,
you're a constant whisper, my purest pride.
In every corner, each dream, every scheme,
forever my home, my dream, my stream.

My preteen daughter

My preteen daughter,
cinnamon skin, playful flare.
Bright, big eyes that gleam,
loving, clever, ever so dear.
My precious gem, heaven's dream.

With her smile so sweet,
my day she lights anew.
Glows like when the morning sun takes its seat,
spirit free, each day she'll renew.
She's growing, though she may change.

She'll always be my girl.
My light in shadow's dark,
forever free to dance and twirl,
to be who she aims to embark,
bringing joy, a bond so stark.

My Valentine Princess

As the twilight of my days does bend,
a divine gift touches my age's blend,
a princess with eyes of night's own hue,
mirror of cosmos, her gaze imbued.

Her skin, a canvas of Latin verse so fine,
hair by the moon softly entwined,
within them, the night's secrets lie deep,
subtle notes of darkness her destinies keep.

My girl's love, a sweet and luminous chant,
beneath the tree of life, time can't supplant,
with gentle hands and a heart so pure,
she's the living verse, sacred and sure.

In the sparkle of her laughter, my cheer is found,
love's tender breeze, so innocent, unbound,
for her, reaching the sky feels so slight,
a dreamer's dream, beyond night's flight.

Through seasons time can't resist,
laughter finds pure joy in her midst,
pure and innocent as first love's glow,
my vast dreams in her small glow grow.

Ten springs she's lived, love aglow and tall,
on love's day, her breath, full of love's call,
my life and hers, an unbreakable tie,
a treasure incomparable in love's sky.

Born radiant and strong, like a shield's acclaim,
today, a sweet day of hearts aflame,
my heart entwined with my girl so dear,
a gift from God, all make clear!

My Own Essence

On the canvas of life, being is a grand art,
my essence shines strong, an original spark.
It's me, my laughter in the wind, no masks in sight,
weaving with starlight my clear and true light.

With my being I weave melodies, happiness by my side,
sailing an ocean of smiles, in harmony we glide.
Comfortable with close souls, like waves in their flow,
my presence asks nothing, just says, "let's go."

I'm unbridled laughter, light without a bind,
gravitating through the cosmos, no route confined.
In Life's symphony, I'm joyful, I'm first,
enjoying each sky, where darkness is nursed.

With a heart full of harmony and jubilant tone,
along joy's path, I mark my astral zone.
Happiness is my flag, proudly it's shaken,
in Life's concert, I've always partaken.

In my existence, I seek solace among the flowers,
at ease with those around me, sharing my colors' powers.
I'm a comforting breeze on days of harsh sun's glare,
embracing silence at night, in the dark's bare.

Triumphs of others don't cloud my lens,
each triumph I celebrate, no holds or bends.
Generosity in me, a vast and deep space,
where every star shines, without a world race.

I don't covet another's peak conquered with might,
my steps dance to my internal rhythms just right.
I know my worth in this unscripted play,
no desire for others' applause, mine's the only ray.

In my chest lies a treasure, of pure and eternal gain,
I suffice and excel in love's fraternal reign.
I look in the mirror with a modern wink,
to that 'self' not needing another's link.

The voice of my heart, with no fear, I let fly,
like a breeze gently caressing, with no intention to tie.
My words are birds wishing to dance and rhyme,
saying in free flight, "To be me is love's prime."

I seek not acceptance, nor yield to the outside crowd,
my joy doesn't rely on approval, self-sufficiency is loud.
Freedom lives within my spirit, no weight to smother,
expressing each truth, my modern creed's cover.

My essence doesn't feed on acceptance's bread,
not looking for another's verdict in my head.
In what I think and feel, my voice is sought,
like a bird in free flight, my choices fraught.

Pure essence, undiluted, not born to conceal,
the acceptance of other worlds I don't appeal.
Living the life, I paint with authenticity high,
my soul seeks no mirrors, in others clarity lie.

I'm a being of worth, doubt has not grazed my way,
My value is a stigma of what I've sown, my display.
Like a tree rooted deep in its very core,
My esteem is the sap that my trunk does store.

Others' triumphs I celebrate, a rain in the garden,
cultivating in a foreign land, from within begotten.
I'm peace in the storm, an embrace in sorrow's fold,
my being, divine temperance, seeks in all its gold.

Firm self-recognition, my mirror, loyal mentor,
I value myself with a sincere 'I love you', with splendor.
I deliver my voice to the world, my thoughts, my feel,
this is who I am, not in shadows, in light, to reveal.

In the expression of my mind, transparent, no inaction,
my soul doesn't play games, says "here I am" in traction.
I'm the sea that whispers its secrets, to the shore nonstop,
with truth that doesn't dry, nor fears debris atop.

Though change is a companion in my earthly voyage,
there's a fire that in me persists, an immortal carriage.
An unbreakable essence, a seal that knows no end,
I am me, this is my essence, in every verse, my friend.

May my essence not bend, not sell, nor give away,
a beacon that lights, beyond the darkest day.
In sea of thousand destinies, my boat knows me well,
a poet of life, whose essence will always dwell.

My American Oak Tree

In the depths of my yard, it rises tall and still,
a young American oak, gripping the land's fill.
Its roots run deep, grappling with eternity,
its canopy challenges the sky with authority.

Fertile, each seed a promise of new ascent,
its leaves whisper softness, in judicious consent,
a song of power deeply rooted, unwaveringly bold,
dwelling in honesty, in every crevice, untold.

Thus, to my American oak, I pay my respect,
an immortal monarch in my garden, a witness direct.
Beneath its shade, life drifts and time is but a trek,
on its green throne, the sun surrenders, its high check.

Sunset love

It hurts to dream of you in my leave,
sorrowful, erasing my return's reprieve,
reflecting a peace that's merely a guise,
like a kiss that's not a true prize.

I depart still thinking I hold you dear,
with the complaint of a dying flame near,
a void so vast, it leads to an end,
a weeping that chokes, refusing to bend.

Eyes of Caribbean Sun

Her eyes of Caribbean Sun,
melt my skin of ice, I come undone.
My soul trembles when they shine,
and if they don't, I feel like dying.

Springs ultimately end

Beneath a mourning sky, this chant I send,
for young teens by monsters met their end.
Sent forth to seek knowledge and allure,
they found on their path shadows impure.

In dark corners of a sacred abode,
where love should be a refuge, a code,
evil lurks, disturbing the peace,
snuffing out young lives, sorrow does release.

What twisted mind can innocence impair?
Can joy be torn by the futures unfair?
The echo of pain in the city resounds,
pleading divine clarity, where evil abounds.

In His infinite mystery, can God console?
Faced with the void left by a star's toll.
Is there just punishment for such disdain?
A nation mourns its daughters, seek balm for the pain.

Only in a fallen world, in shadows deep set,
such vile cruelty, such cruel fate begets.
You, divine deity, in your starry cloak of light,
comfort the people, the hearts in plight.

For each life cut short, a flower we'll sow,
for each future stolen, their memory will show.
In a garden of remembrance, of pain transformed,
may light reach the soul, the father so mourned.

May these flowers be light, renewed hope to find,
for the shattered parents in their souls confined.
May each petal, each scent, remind,
of our daughters lost, springs left behind.

With every flower planted, a vow we make,
to fight for a tomorrow where evil we break,
where our girls grow up without fear's cruel hand,
and in each homecoming, only love will stand.

Let's seek to fill the void in every heart,
for each lost flower, which brings us apart.
May in every petal reborn be lost hope,
and in our souls, let strength and courage be their cope.

These verses pay tribute to lives cut short,
of stolen springs, tears we've brought.
For each lost girl, a flower in her name,
to remember her life, her struggle, her flame.

Desire's Embrace

I want to make love to you,
in torrents of sweat that ensue.
In whirlwinds of sighs unbound,
amid the sweet sound
of my trembling frame,
bursting in the melody's claim
of your primal cries profound.

I want to make love to you,
sliding down your hills so true,
resting between your valleys deep,
hidden in hollows you keep,
of that chest inclining graciously
to receive the heartfelt plea.
I want to make love to you.

Feel the softness of your hair,
disperse amidst my fingers with care.
The grooves of your lips so sweet,
to calm within mine's discreet,
and ultimately explode within your core
with the force of a roaring roar,
foamy torrent from my stream's secretes.

Memories

Because memories exist, they remain to stay,
sometimes you cry for all the good days,
or cry for sad moments that have cost,
yearning for those who've left, those who're lost.

Sea Blooming Rose

My Sea Blooming Rose,
awake I know you dance,
the day lit up by your vibrant glance.
The sun, yet sleeping, soon will beam,
showing its might, its fiery gleam.
I fear its envy, blooming Rose.
Never look at it. Without your eyes,
I will die.

Shadow the Blue Merle Madame

At the threshold lies Shadow, Blue Merle's dear grace,
guardian of glances, two moons set in place.
Eyes like spheres of the dimly lit night in twine.
Her loyalty shines of one so pure and so fine.

Languid traits on her face, calmness whispers below,
reflecting her soul, like a serene sea's glow. Unconditional
waiting, as patient as a sage,
in her noble demeanor, love forms a foreign stage.

Silent as I depart, her heart stays awake,
nostalgia in her chest, she subtly guard's.
Longing for the door to break, my form to appear.

And upon my return, emotions overflow clear.
Her jumps turn to poetry, celebrating my arrival, so dear.
Without Shadow, loyal friend, my will would break.

Ode to a Kindred Soul

Beside you, my friend, in paths and trails, so true,
we share the earth, the sky, the wind's gentle view,
each step we take, a bond, a firm path we mend,
of endless adventures, joyful and tender blend.

In the quiet rustle of tender leaves so fair,
our friendship found its birth, its loving care,
and amidst laughter and talks, we find our cheer,
in foliage and river, we create legends we hold dear.

Strong against adversity, we boldly rise,
our dreams stand, two souls in fierce, shared guise.
For in battle, our bond is what we wear.

Your loyalty's a beacon, you hold me near,
in tests of integrity, your female voice so kind and clear,
without the harsh betrayal of friendships insincere.

Humid Dreams

In the dark veil of the night's space,
in Morpheus' realm, a desire takes place,
alert in the young body's eager delight,
woven with passion in its gleaming light.

Puberty paints with its gentle brush,
on the night canvas, a soft-hued blush,
delights of an unnamed, secretive Eden,
caresses of a whisper, though hidden.

Pulse quickens in the shadows' embrace,
young heart dazzled by love's gentle grace.
Dawn brings a bright awakening morn,
mind finds calm in the tide reborn.

Heart beats in its own rhythmic sway,
in dormant ecstasy, where dreams lay,
Humid dreams arrive, a sweet burst of play,
vivid, playful, in a wild display.

Wings unfold, a tender bond to keep,
mind weaves fantasies, felt too deep,
heart gallops lively in the morning's leap,
after the sweet dreams from the night's sleep.

A love that withers

In the abyss where the heart cries,
lies my feeling, desolate, in sighs.
In an ocean of unrequited love's plight,
I weep for love fading from sight.

Though wounded, I won't give up the fight,
hope still my beacon, shining bright.
Despite the sorrow and painful divide,
I'll cling to love, though lost in the tide.

In nights of torment, solitude's cold bide,
I seek in each star a blessing to find,
and in each dream, a new truth to confide.
Even in feared oblivion, love I want to make mine.

In the shadow of vast, unending solitude,
my heart whispers your name with tender grace,
longing for a secure love, not one that eludes.
Why does your distant echo show no trace?

I wish to be ivy, clinging close to you,
not to relinquish, though sadness accrues,
a river of tears reflects my misgivings,
of an ardor unwavering, that never stops giving.

Still, I refuse to let passion wane,
to rekindle a sweet love, free from disdain,
where this unconditional love may reign.

I cling to hope in fervent resist,
won't surrender, my love shall insist,
still yearning for a love that no longer exists.

Vienna in a Waltz's Whisper

Beneath an emperor's blue sky's grace,
Vienna rests in a gentle waltz's embrace,
Schubert's breath in resplendent flow,
A classic pulse in its veins aglow.

In air-filled cathedrals, the empire unfurls,
centuries old coffee, the aroma swirls,
where Freud, dreaming, etches the mind,
a Vienna that thinks, feels, and virtue finds.

Perhaps Freud walked these streets profound,
cartographing minds like a map of stars, around,
in coffee houses, conversations move free,
as the Danube kisses its ancient reverie.

Celtic heritage beats in its heart,
Vedunia's whisper in winds apart,
voices from origins ardently proclaim,
stones forming its steadfast frame.

Vienna, oh Vienna, pristine and grand,
Your beauty weaves through the urban land,
in your streets and squares, art sings loud,
within your culture, the world stands proud.

Your palaces hold secrets untold,
Hofburg stands regal, it's history bold,
rooms harboring imperial dreams enfold,
opulence and art in its manifold.

Graceful avenues, gardens finessed,
architecture challenging skies with no rest,
each building a stone-crafted tale,
quality of life in each day's inhale.

In sweet memory, the apfelstrudel's prize,
layers of sweetness interlaced and wise,
like Viennese life, rich in hue,
ancestor's feast, skillfully spiced through and through.

The Vienna Boys' Choir, celestial tones,
angels' chorus, in sacred zones,
little seraphs defying time's stride,
in their songs, genius' pride.

In your legacy, in pride you stand,
a portrait of eras etched by hand,
you're music, history, and confection pure,
in Europe's heart, Vienna's allure.

Epilogue

In this poetry collection "Odes to Life," each verse is like a stroke on the canvas of existence, capturing moments, emotions, and reflections with a poetic depth that invites contemplation and emotional connection. Through this mosaic of words, I, the author, weave a tapestry of experiences, allegories, and metaphors that shed light on the complexity of human life, from moments of love and beauty to challenges and losses. Each verse echoes the very essence of existence, exploring universal themes such as love, freedom, nostalgia, suffering, political struggles, and identity.

"Odes to Life," is poetry that becomes a torrent of flowing emotions, immersing the reader in landscapes of thought and feeling. The verses are windows to a vast universe of meanings and symbolisms, where every word is chosen to convey a particular truth or emotion. Through the richness and complexity of these stanzas, I invite reflection on the fleeting nature of life, the beauty of encounters and goodbyes, the strength of love, and the hope that shines amid darkness.

End of poetry.

About the Author

Nicolás Muñoz, distinguished for his notable career as a university professor of economics and government, renowned columnist, and expert consultant in management, finance, and education, has transcended academic and professional boundaries to delve into the vibrant world of literature. He has not only contributed six texts on economics, government, personal finance, and values, but has also explored poetry. For him, poetry is not just a hobby but a channel to express his deepest reflections on life, society, philosophy, intense human passions, and his love for nature.

He is a dedicated husband and father of three children, two sons and a daughter, who are a constant source of inspiration for his writing. The publication of his first collection of poems marks the beginning of a new stage in his career as a writer and his deep interest in poetry as a form of art and personal expression.

The End